The Most Powerful Quotes and Affirmations From the Heart

Inspirational, Motivational, and Empowering
Words for Growth and Happiness

Kala Jordan-Lindsey

The Most Powerful Quotes & Affirmations From the Heart: Inspirational, Motivational, and Empowering Words for Growth and Happiness

Copyright @ 2024 by Kala Jordan-Lindsey

All rights reserved. No portion of this book may be reproduced or utilized in any form or by any means, electronic or mechanical, including photocopying, recording, or by any other information storage and retrieval system, without permission in writing from the author.

Disclaimer Notice:

Please note the information in this book is for informational purposes only. The reader should regularly consult a physician in matters relating to his/her overall health and particularly with respect to any symptoms that may require diagnosis or medical attention.

The views expressed are those of the author and should not be taken as expert instruction or commands. The reader is responsible for his or her own actions.

Adherence to all applicable laws and regulations, including international, federal, state, and local governing professional licensing, business practices, advertising, and all other aspects of doing business in the US, Canada, or any other jurisdiction is the sole responsibility of the reader.

The author does not assume any responsibility or liability whatsoever on the behalf of the reader of this material.

Cover Design by Goran Tovilovic
Interior Design by Goran Tovilovic
Photo Credit: Kala Jordan-Lindsey
Editor: Sana Abuleil

www.kalajordanlindsey.com
Please send inquiries to Write@kalajordanlindsey.com

DEDICATION

This book is dedicated to myself, for having the guts and motivation to release words I could not hold within.

This book is dedicated to my husband, Anthony, and our beautiful daughter, Kamaria, for being an inspiration behind writing and completing this book.

This book is dedicated to my parents, Jefferson and Evella, for being two of my biggest fans, who never stopped believing in me.

This book is also dedicated to my close friend, Belinda Arzella Dalton, for inspiring me to publish more encouraging and inspirational words.

And this book is dedicated to those who walked away with a signed copy of "The Most Powerful Quotes to Enhance Your Life" at the Northway Wellness Center in Miami, Florida. You inspired me to release another one. May "The Most Powerful Quotes & Affirmations From the Heart" offer you and those who read it the perfect words to enhance your life and help you flourish successfully.

TABLE OF CONTENTS

Introduction 6

How to Get the Most Out of This Book 8

The Most Powerful Quotes From the Heart 13

The Most Powerful Affirmations From the Heart 95

Acknowledgements 99

Other books by Kala Jordan-Lindsey 102

INTRODUCTION

The Most Powerful Quotes and Affirmations From the Heart by Kala Jordan-Lindsey is a deeply inspirational collection of motivational quotes and affirmations designed to uplift, empower, and encourage readers to embrace personal growth and faith, which leads one to discover true happiness. Through heartfelt words, the author invites readers to reflect on the challenges and triumphs of life, while offering wisdom on perseverance, resilience, and the importance of allowing God to be our guide. The book blends practical advice with spiritual belief, providing insights into embracing change, overcoming adversity, and finding one's true purpose and calling. It is a source of inspiration for those seeking to thrive in their personal and spiritual lives, needing that extra nudge to keep moving forward.

Some of these quotations are meant to inspire you, some to offer you wisdom, some to open your eyes, and even some to calm your heart. But all of these quotations are meant to encourage you in your everyday life with words that will help you flourish successfully—one day at a time.

So, take your time and digest each quotation with a grateful and open heart. Let this book motivate you to participate in and celebrate your growth journey while living on purpose. You can do it. It's short, sweet, and worth the reading experience.

Thank you,
Kala Jordan-Lindsey

How to Get the Most Out of This Book

This book has been created to work in several ways:

1. It's an unlimited day journey that you can start at any time, but consistency is important. Read one quotation a day, and allow that quotation to encourage you for the entire day. Write it down, carry it with you, and read it as often as needed. Take a few minutes and write down any thoughts or feelings you have about it. You will be amazed at the immediate impact you can experience with this process.

2. You may read this book like any other by letting it do the following: inhale and exhale after meditating on a quotation or two. Let it resonate in your mind as you reflect on its positive meaning. Taste it as you embrace the physical experience, and observe a moment of silence as you reflect on the quotation(s).

3. You may choose a quotation and journal about how it applies to your life, or go the extra mile and even write a book about it.

4. You may create a vision board or video as a reference for encouragement, or place each quotation in a glass jar or shoebox so you can pick one out each day to meditate on and embrace.

5. Have fun and enjoy this book! Share it with family, friends, and loved ones, and even strangers—you never know whose life you'll touch by doing something small, but big in God's eyes.

You will succeed when you make time to embrace your steps of life with purpose and with a positive attitude.

-Kala Jordan-Lindsey

Your failures aren't bad.
They are lessons to learn
from to help you improve
and win, every time.

-Kala Jordan-Lindsey

The right direction will always lead you to success if you don't become distracted and discouraged during uncontrollable circumstances.

-Kala Jordan-Lindsey

The Most Powerful Quotes From the Heart

If you want to be on top, get there. Do what it takes to be in the position where you desire to be no matter how long it takes you to reach this spot. And never give up.

- Kala Jordan - Lindsey

Grace will always outweigh your "nos" in life. So embrace rejection.

- Kala Jordan - Lindsey

Sometimes, God will send you in a new direction to meet great and friendly people that will touch your life.

- Kala Jordan - Lindsey

There's nothing wrong with change when you're confident you're going in the right direction.

- Kala Jordan - Lindsey

Wise living is key to success.

-Kala Jordan-Lindsey

You're blossoming in the image of a flower—beautifully.

-Kala Jordan-Lindsey

When heartbreaking words distract your moments, think about the goodness and grace of Jesus.

-Kala Jordan-Lindsey

You can overcome bad habits if you choose to.

-Kala Jordan-Lindsey

A moment of silence can be powerful if you know how to embrace it.

-Kala Jordan-Lindsey

Your ability moves others to strive and triumph.

-Kala Jordan-Lindsey

Repeated good habits are contagious and inspire others.

- Kala Jordan - Lindsey

Uncommon opportunities have the potential to lead to great success.

- Kala Jordan - Lindsey

Writing books allows you to escape the real world and create magical stories of a life you desire to live.

- Kala Jordan - Lindsey

Your calling gives you access to doors others won't enter.

- Kala Jordan-Lindsey

Love is bigger than the size of your heart and more powerful than your imagination.

- Kala Jordan-Lindsey

You're built with a creative imagination. Use it.

- Kala Jordan-Lindsey

Strive to discover Life, and you'll discover your real purpose for living.

-Kala Jordan-Lindsey

It's not over until you no longer exist. Expect a door to open sooner or later.

-Kala Jordan-Lindsey

Denial prepares you for grace and another door of opportunity.

-Kala Jordan-Lindsey

You shine everywhere you go and when you speak.

-Kala Jordan-Lindsey

Many will congratulate you without supporting you. But those who do, cherish your relationship with them.

-Kala Jordan-Lindsey

When you escape your desires, you'll discover what satisfies your soul.

-Kala Jordan-Lindsey

There's always a bright side in a dark season. Search for the Light and embrace Him at all times.

-Kala Jordan-Lindsey

A person who is determined to win will always find ways to overcome life.

-Kala Jordan-Lindsey

When you climb with faith, you'll make it to the top.

-Kala Jordan-Lindsey

You don't need an opportunity to create one.
You are the door. Initiate it.

-Kala Jordan-Lindsey

Just because people "like" you on social media
doesn't mean they love you in person.

-Kala Jordan-Lindsey

Doing it alone isn't a bad thing. You get to keep
a hundred pieces of pie.

-Kala Jordan-Lindsey

A new direction isn't good luck. It's planned grace.

-Kala Jordan-Lindsey

Change helps you get closer to your destination.

-Kala Jordan-Lindsey

You're going somewhere incredible, no matter what you're going through. Embrace the journey until you get there.

-Kala Jordan-Lindsey

Sometimes, to accomplish a goal you have to do something uncommon, take a risk with faith, or do what others fear with unapologetic confidence.

- Kala Jordan-Lindsey

You don't have to stay down. When you rise, perform your passion and others will be inspired to do the same.

- Kala Jordan-Lindsey

Doing something over and over can be boring unless you do it with purpose.

-Kala Jordan-Lindsey

You possess the ability to overcome bad thoughts when you refuse to let them enter your space.

-Kala Jordan-Lindsey

Reading empowers you to discover great things, and writing gives you the freedom to live.

-Kala Jordan-Lindsey

Pursue God, and you would never have to chase man.

- Kala Jordan-Lindsey

One step prepares you for many successful moves.

- Kala Jordan-Lindsey

Love living, and you'll feel more confident about your walk.

- Kala Jordan-Lindsey

Living is more satisfying than just being alive.

-Kala Jordan-Lindsey

False love is toxic. True love is real.

-Kala Jordan-Lindsey

Failure leads to a turning point. Be optimistic when it happens.

-Kala Jordan-Lindsey

When you choose to stand on your feet, you have the opportunity to make a difference.

-Kala Jordan-Lindsey

When you find your drive for a living, you gain an understanding of uncontrollable life events.

-Kala Jordan-Lindsey

Choose your lifestyle or let the world create it for you.

-Kala Jordan-Lindsey

God has the power to clean up your mess without you sweeping.

-Kala Jordan-Lindsey

Life isn't about how many times you win a fight. It's about your resilience to never give up and embrace whatever comes your way.

-Kala Jordan-Lindsey

Contacts may fade away, but a loyal friend will remain near your side through thick and thin.

-Kala Jordan-Lindsey

Starting at square one is better than giving up. Life is a beautiful blessing but meaningless until you start living.

-Kala Jordan-Lindsey

Falling in love is better than dreaming.

-Kala Jordan-Lindsey

A new direction isn't good luck. It's a planned grace and a door to discover your destiny.

-Kala Jordan-Lindsey

Your faith will give you access to doors others can't enter and opportunities that will change your life.

-Kala Jordan-Lindsey

Holding in stuff will clog your heart until you let go and empty everything unhealthy in your life.

-Kala Jordan-Lindsey

When you discover your calling, your perspective about life will change.

-Kala Jordan-Lindsey

Successful habits are contagious.

-Kala Jordan-Lindsey

When you let go of your life, great things will happen; you'll discover blessings you never imagined.

-Kala Jordan-Lindsey

Reading helps you live, and reveals secrets to help you thrive boldly and do more than you could imagine.

-Kala Jordan-Lindsey

Problems are solvable by the power and grace of God.

-Kala Jordan-Lindsey

Change keeps you on track and gets you closer to where you need to be in life.

-Kala Jordan-Lindsey

Success happens when you are determined to experience the reality of your goals.

-Kala Jordan-Lindsey

If you want to accomplish something, you have to start somewhere and be determined to never give up.

- Kala Jordan-Lindsey

Discover God, and you'll find true happiness for real.

- Kala Jordan-Lindsey

If you roll with Jesus, He'll never let you down.

- Kala Jordan-Lindsey

The right way will be wrong to someone else so follow the Spirit of God and you'll never go wrong.

-Kala Jordan-Lindsey

Great things happen when you show up and execute with confidence.

-Kala Jordan-Lindsey

Living empowers you to know things that are hidden from others.

-Kala Jordan-Lindsey

Life is worth finding while you're breathing.

-Kala Jordan-Lindsey

If you don't view your situations from a spiritual standpoint, storms may freak you out.

-Kala Jordan-Lindsey

Don't be so corporate where you forget about being human.

-Kala Jordan-Lindsey

Change lets you see the good and bigger picture in your shift.

-Kala Jordan-Lindsey

A wandering mind is bound to distract your focus on the important things of life.

-Kala Jordan-Lindsey

Invite peace into your environment and you'll accomplish things.

-Kala Jordan-Lindsey

Being greedy isn't healthy if you have enough to share with others.

- Kala Jordan - Lindsey

You can create magic on the page unlike a magician.

- Kala Jordan - Lindsey

After you stop wrestling with your flesh, God will grace you with divine power to start living.

- Kala Jordan - Lindsey

Climb, no matter how difficult the mountain looks. There is hope wherever you are on your journey.

-Kala Jordan-Lindsey

It's okay to dream until you find your passion.

-Kala Jordan-Lindsey

Writing a book tears you apart and exposes everything your soul hungers to release to help others.

-Kala Jordan-Lindsey

If you don't get the opportunity, don't fret and be discouraged. Create it.

— Kala Jordan-Lindsey

Denials open doors of blessings and discovery.

— Kala Jordan-Lindsey

When you have a goal and set your mind to it despite adversity, you'll succeed.

— Kala Jordan-Lindsey

When your spouse asks for a tip, give him lots of love.

-Kala Jordan-Lindsey

Everything you see isn't always good for you but whatever comes your way is a gift from God.

-Kala Jordan-Lindsey

Those hungry will find a way to eat and motivate others along the way.

-Kala Jordan-Lindsey

Dig deep, and you'll find what you need and more.

- Kala Jordan-Lindsey

When you discover your voice, you can do what you want.

- Kala Jordan-Lindsey

You're approved without a confirmation.

- Kala Jordan-Lindsey

Sometimes, a breakthrough will follow a battle.

-Kala Jordan-Lindsey

The Light is in your valley even when you don't think so.

-Kala Jordan-Lindsey

Your hands have the power to create something no one else will develop.

-Kala Jordan-Lindsey

Growth is when you're able to smile and keep moving after all the ups and downs you've experienced.

-Kala Jordan-Lindsey

It's hard to find the right man when your heart is pursuing the one you don't need.

-Kala Jordan-Lindsey

You're becoming your best version each day. Keep going. You're growing.

-Kala Jordan-Lindsey

Your calling has nothing to do with your zip code. God has the power to grace you wherever you are.

-Kala Jordan-Lindsey

Being an author doesn't mean you're perfect. It gives you the blessing and freedom to share with others about your imperfect life.

-Kala Jordan-Lindsey

Keep going. You're growing. You're becoming your best version each day.

-Kala Jordan-Lindsey

When insecurities run your life and dictate your thoughts, your hope and faith become weak.

- Kala Jordan-Lindsey

You have the authority to do great things and impact many lives. Discover your voice and embrace it.

- Kala Jordan-Lindsey

Think positive. You don't have to let your negative thoughts run your life and block you from moving forward.

- Kala Jordan-Lindsey

When you overcome your toxic mindset, you'll discover confidence and win.

-Kala Jordan-Lindsey

Your greatest secrets are power for your neighbors.

-Kala Jordan-Lindsey

The truth about being human is that you are not alone.

-Kala Jordan-Lindsey

Your confidence is connected to your purpose and calling.

-Kala Jordan-Lindsey

You're history for generations to come.

-Kala Jordan-Lindsey

Life is meaningless until you discover your purpose and embrace your calling.

-Kala Jordan-Lindsey

Knowing the value of money is more important than earning and spending it.

-Kala Jordan-Lindsey

Many people know you but not everyone desires to have a relationship with you. Be careful not to get your feelings hurt.

-Kala Jordan-Lindsey

Your future is bright. Focus on getting there one day at a time.

-Kala Jordan-Lindsey

Life is not about money but understanding the discipline of it.

-Kala Jordan-Lindsey

The extra mile you take will help you succeed.

-Kala Jordan-Lindsey

Trees blossom just as your heart.

-Kala Jordan-Lindsey

Your imagination has the power to create an incredible book.

-Kala Jordan-Lindsey

You don't need a crowd of individuals to help you succeed. Yourself plus God is enough.

-Kala Jordan-Lindsey

Life isn't easy, but you don't have to live yours like your neighbor.

-Kala Jordan-Lindsey

Going the extra mile is purposeless unless you have a reason why you're doing what others will not do.

-Kala Jordan-Lindsey

Your address doesn't define your abilities nor future.

-Kala Jordan-Lindsey

When you create a life with God, great things will happen that you never experienced in the past.

-Kala Jordan-Lindsey

Don't allow your situation today to hinder your tomorrow.

-Kala Jordan-Lindsey

Sometimes, God will let you experience an uncomfortable life storm to shift you into a satisfying position.

-Kala Jordan-Lindsey

The worst thing ever could turn out to be the best thing that could have ever happened in your life.

-Kala Jordan-Lindsey

Love and kindness create happiness.

-Kala Jordan-Lindsey

Your enemies will bless you when you least expect them to.

-Kala Jordan-Lindsey

Letting go of untold words on paper can take years to accomplish, like a healing journey; sharing your stories with others isn't always a quick and easy process for many, but when you're brave enough to go for it, it's fulfilling and empowers you to discover the path and secrets to living.

-Kala Jordan-Lindsey

Your greatest turn will be the most powerful one that changes your life and others.

-Kala Jordan-Lindsey

It takes courage to climb an unfamiliar mountain and build from the bottom.

-Kala Jordan-Lindsey

Having faith gives you courage to follow your calling with no regrets.

-Kala Jordan-Lindsey

Differences that unite with love and peace help improve the world.

-Kala Jordan-Lindsey

Your chances of succeeding are greater than your fears.

-Kala Jordan-Lindsey

You don't need to know everything to create something worth an eye.

-Kala Jordan-Lindsey

Confidence is everything—never lose it, but find ways to share it with others.

—Kala Jordan-Lindsey

You don't need a lot to make a big difference in the world. Write a book from within, and you will inspire many.

—Kala Jordan-Lindsey

Your greatest potential has the power to inspire lives and bless those who are hopeless.

—Kala Jordan-Lindsey

Writing a book takes courage, especially when it's challenging. But it's possible.

- Kala Jordan - Lindsey

Change is never easy but there is hope wherever the wind takes you.

- Kala Jordan - Lindsey

Build with Jesus, and you'll never go out of business.

- Kala Jordan - Lindsey

You can't wear a mask your whole life if you want to live; wearing makeup only lasts for so long.

-Kala Jordan-Lindsey

Sometimes, God will reveal your purpose in unusual situations for a greater reason beyond your imagination. Your passion will never leave you alone.

-Kala Jordan-Lindsey

Sometimes, you have to experience a life storm to reach your destination.

-Kala Jordan-Lindsey

Working hard will make you happy, but working smart will fulfill your mind, body, and soul.

-Kala Jordan-Lindsey

When you accomplish something it feels good. But when you know it was only by the grace of God, it humbles you.

-Kala Jordan-Lindsey

You'll win. Follow the Leader.

-Kala Jordan-Lindsey

Accomplishing a goal feels good, but it takes work to achieve it.

-Kala Jordan-Lindsey

Have faith despite what you think you can't do. Put your mind to it and go for it, like aiming for a three on the basketball court.

-Kala Jordan-Lindsey

Following the crowd isn't always good. They just may lead you in the wrong direction.

-Kala Jordan-Lindsey

Be it...happy.

- Kala Jordan-Lindsey

One of the greatest moves you could ever make is the one right now.

- Kala Jordan-Lindsey

When you realize what you need to change to grow and live better than yesterday, do it, embrace it, and never give up on great things to come.

- Kala Jordan-Lindsey

Sometimes, God will open your eyes in the middle of a life storm only to reveal your calling, an extraordinary blessing that is more powerful than the disturbance if you have faith.

-Kala Jordan-Lindsey

\What you think you can't do may be the greatest thing you ever accomplish.

-Kala Jordan-Lindsey

When you have faith and push through the most difficult situations in life, you'll begin to grow.

-Kala Jordan-Lindsey

Sometimes, you have to change your atmosphere to grow.

-Kala Jordan-Lindsey

It's easy to abandon your mind when you don't know how to embrace it with wisdom, positive thoughts, and discipline.

-Kala Jordan-Lindsey

When you have hope, your faith will make it happen.

-Kala Jordan-Lindsey

A race isn't worth it if you're doing it for the wrong reasons.

-Kala Jordan-Lindsey

Step into your purpose, and you'll have more reasons to live more than ever.

-Kala Jordan-Lindsey

If you let God change your mind, you could do more than you imagine without a doubt.

-Kala Jordan-Lindsey

It's never too early or late to encourage someone. We all struggle, so we all need encouragement.

- Kala Jordan-Lindsey

You can build anything from scratch, but without faith, it will not be as successful as it could be.

- Kala Jordan-Lindsey

You'll only know who needs encouragement once you are the light.

- Kala Jordan-Lindsey

Losing something isn't the pain. It's the memories that hurt the most.

- Kala Jordan-Lindsey

Doubt will cause you to miss the train. Have faith, and it'll arrive.

- Kala Jordan-Lindsey

You are your biggest setback. Let loose and live.

- Kala Jordan-Lindsey

If at first you don't succeed, you'll win the next time you try again.

- Kala Jordan-Lindsey

When you desire to make wiser choices, your life will also change.

- Kala Jordan-Lindsey

If you're trying to get somewhere in life, keep going and striving one day at a time.

- Kala Jordan-Lindsey

Live before your next breath.

-Kala Jordan-Lindsey

A healthier life will make you happier.

-Kala Jordan-Lindsey

It's okay to face your reality. It's harder not to, so be courageous and do it.

-Kala Jordan-Lindsey

When you run into challenging circumstances, don't focus on the problem. Instead, focus on overcoming obstacles with a positive attitude fueled by faith.

-Kala Jordan-Lindsey

Love your hands because you know what they can do.

-Kala Jordan-Lindsey

If you think the storm you're in is the worst thing ever, know that it could simply be the best thing that could have ever happened in your life.

-Kala Jordan-Lindsey

Success starts with possessing a positive mindset.

-Kala Jordan-Lindsey

Your calling needs you more than your dreams.

-Kala Jordan-Lindsey

Obedience starts with our Heavenly Father.

-Kala Jordan-Lindsey

You can't rest if you always worry about situations out of your hands.

- Kala Jordan-Lindsey

If you ever have trouble doing something, change your mind by making it fun.

- Kala Jordan-Lindsey

Many are doing what you do, but don't worry because there's only one of you.

- Kala Jordan-Lindsey

Life is full of unexpectedness. But when you're prepared to bless others, God will make it happen and continue to grace you to shine your light. Live intentionally.

-Kala Jordan-Lindsey

Stepping out on faith will open doors for you. Giving up will not. So, wherever you are on your journey, have faith even when it "seems" like things aren't moving or working out in your favor.

-Kala Jordan-Lindsey

God knows best and never makes mistakes.

-Kala Jordan-Lindsey

A new chapter is never easy. There are a lot of unexpectedness and hurdles you may experience and moments that you become discouraged. But staying focused and prayerful through it all helps you to appreciate God's favor in your life; His grace and mercy, and love will keep you satisfied no matter what fight you face.

-Kala Jordan-Lindsey

If you can plant a seed of hope in one brain, you could inspire millions.

-Kala Jordan-Lindsey

The moment you allow fear to enter your thoughts, your faith will stay buried in your heart until you learn to have confidence and trust the Lord over your life.

-Kala Jordan-Lindsey

You can pursue what you want to be, but God will position you where you need to be.

-Kala Jordan-Lindsey

Remember that one mistake or failure doesn't mean it's over. Unexpectedness doesn't just happen without a win sooner or later.

-Kala Jordan-Lindsey

Don't be embarrassed. Let your struggles become your story to inspire others.

-Kala Jordan-Lindsey

You'll never embrace the power you have until you unleash your passion.

-Kala Jordan-Lindsey

Sometimes, God will change your life so He can transform your identity.

- Kala Jordan-Lindsey

Simple, but purposeful adjustments to your lifestyle or in your life have the power to do amazing things.

- Kala Jordan-Lindsey

Live life to the fullest with no regrets.

- Kala Jordan-Lindsey

Sometimes, God will do extraordinary things to an ordinary person. Be patient. You're next.

- Kala Jordan - Lindsey

A person with a noisy heart needs comfort and healing.

- Kala Jordan - Lindsey

If you feel worthless, remember how blessed you are. This book is for you, so let it motivate you in all the many ways the other million don't.

- Kala Jordan - Lindsey

To accomplish a goal is a process, not a race. What God has for you is for you. So, keep climbing wherever you are on the mountain and expect to succeed.

-Kala Jordan-Lindsey

The day you stop climbing the hills of life is when you stop living to reach your full potential.

-Kala Jordan-Lindsey

To accomplish a goal is a process, not a race. So, wherever you are on your journey, keep striving, and never give up.

-Kala Jordan-Lindsey

God is always in the ring if you acknowledge Him.

-Kala Jordan-Lindsey

For every storm you experience, God has a message for you in it.

-Kala Jordan-Lindsey

Behind every smile is someone's story.

-Kala Jordan-Lindsey

Your breakthrough will happen in a blink of an eye, so stay hopeful about your next discovery.

-Kala Jordan-Lindsey

New chapters aren't always easy, but they're necessary for growth.

-Kala Jordan-Lindsey

You have power over your storms, but God *will deliver you.*

-Kala Jordan-Lindsey

When you feel like giving up, think about how far you've come, and keep going.

-Kala Jordan-Lindsey

Getting sidetracked is easy when you're not focused. So, if you're trying to get somewhere, focus on the journey, not the noise.

-Kala Jordan-Lindsey

Worrying about life doesn't solve your issues any quicker than waiting on God to rescue you and deliver you to your destination.

-Kala Jordan-Lindsey

When you feel you have nothing else to give, give more.

-Kala Jordan-Lindsey

The most powerful voice in the room is yours; cherish your mouthpiece.

-Kala Jordan-Lindsey

You don't have to be depressed. Get up and do something great, and smile.

-Kala Jordan-Lindsey

Distractions can hinder your progress. So, if you're trying to get somewhere in life or make it to your destination, know when to close the blinds.

-Kala Jordan-Lindsey

For every closed door, expect God to open a new one. Think positive, and good things will happen.

-Kala Jordan-Lindsey

Some people are night owls, but others will stand up and help, and that's you.

-Kala Jordan-Lindsey

Living in Christ is more powerful than winning the Powerball without faith.

- Kala Jordan-Lindsey

Let it happen. Don't daydream. It's no fun in Fairyland.

- Kala Jordan-Lindsey

If doubt is overpowering your life, remember who's the Boss.

- Kala Jordan-Lindsey

The world worries more than praying.

-Kala Jordan-Lindsey

No matter who you are and where you're at, God can rescue you safely out of a storm.

-Kala Jordan-Lindsey

There's greatness within you ready to make a difference in the world.

-Kala Jordan-Lindsey

You're a boss's girl.

-Kala Jordan-Lindsey

Cook more, and you'll feel better.

-Kala Jordan-Lindsey

A compliment is more impactful than talking behind someone's back.

-Kala Jordan-Lindsey

God will always reveal your best answers if you have faith and seek His guidance.

-Kala Jordan-Lindsey

Achieving goals isn't easy; it takes passion and perseverance to accomplish anything that matters. And sometimes, driving the extra mile is a part of the process.

-Kala Jordan-Lindsey

Wherever you are on the journey, embrace even the obstacles, the highs and lows of life; God knows your destination on the other side of storms.

-Kala Jordan-Lindsey

Boast less, and God will lift you up effortlessly.

- Kala Jordan-Lindsey

The fear holding you back today will imprison you unless you turn to God. He'll bless you with confidence to overcome doubt.

- Kala Jordan-Lindsey

When you're missing, your contagious spirit is hidden.

- Kala Jordan-Lindsey

God's grace is a lifesaver.

-Kala Jordan-Lindsey

Gaining wisdom leads to peace, love, joy, and happiness.

-Kala Jordan-Lindsey

You don't need a degree to publish a book, but you need to be on fire to write one.

-Kala Jordan-Lindsey

When you accomplish goals, celebrate like it's your birthday.

-Kala Jordan-Lindsey

God loves you more than you love your valuables.

-Kala Jordan-Lindsey

Pain can't be covered unless you're struggling in darkness.

-Kala Jordan-Lindsey

Mistakes allow you to do better and grow.

-Kala Jordan-Lindsey

Embrace the Light of grace and mercy; see the blessing and, more important, purpose in your difficulties.

-Kala Jordan-Lindsey

While you embrace your confidence, look into the mirror and say...

The Most Powerful Affirmations From the Heart

\# I will do better than yesterday and be wiser than my mistakes.

\# I will not let discouragement and denial take over my life.

\# I am brave and will overcome my struggles.

\# I will stay focused like a lion chasing his predictor.

\# I can control my gallery of thoughts with the strength of the Lord.

\# I am stronger than my past.

\# I will climb higher than my rock bottom and succeed.

\# I will make it big one day without fame, fortune, and a million followers.

\# I will soar with faith and grace successfully.

\# I am more intelligent than the world thinks.

\# I can do anything I set my mind to without a team of nonsupporters.

\# I am unique and blessed.

\# I can do the opposite of what doubt tells me.

\# I am creative as an artist.

\# I will conquer my giants.

\# I am better than my past.

\# I am highly favored.

\# I will not let doubt get the best of me.

\# I am unstoppable with my God.

\# I will overcome my list of problems one day at a time.

\# I will achieve more than my intuition tells me.

\# I am enough because my God is mighty.

\# I got this with confidence.

\# I have the ability to persevere with faith.

\# I was created intelligent and highly favored.

\# I will rise when I'm down and succeed like never before.

\# I am smarter than my mobile phone.

\# I am beautiful without makeup.

\# I am confident without confirmation from social media.

\# I will do my very best every time.

\# I naturally inspire and empower others when I shine my light.

Acknowledgements

To my Heavenly Father, who made this all possible. Thank you for your grace, mercy, strength, and love on this journey of releasing another part of my heart and imagination—for helping me release another book from my soul.

To my publishing team and amazing editor, thank you for reading and responding to my emails past midnight and on holidays. Your sincere support, guidance, and professionalism continue to motivate me to work with you.

To my family, friends, and faithful readers and fans, thank you from the bottom of my heart with arms of love as big as the universe for choosing to purchase and read my inspirational works, and share them with others.

Guess what? I have more books on the way, and you want to see the news before the world sees it. For exclusive emails, sign up at www.kalajordanlindsey.com and click submit.

And one more thing: If you were inspired or encouraged during your reading experience, I would love for you to share your feedback. Please visit or click the links below and post your comments on Amazon and Barnes & Noble. I appreciate you. Thanks a million!

Amazon.com: Kala Jordan-Lindsey: books, biography, latest update

Kala Jordan Lindsey | Barnes & Noble®

OTHER BOOKS BY KALA JORDAN-LINDSEY INCLUDE

The Turning Point: Memoirs of Determination, Hope, Faith, Loss, Love, and Resilience

The Most Powerful Quotes to Enhance Your Life: Inspirational and Motivational Quotations to Strengthen Your Mental, Physical, and Spiritual Health

Words From the Heart: Second Edition

Words From the Heart: First Edition

When You Rise: A Poem of Motivation

When You Rise: A Powerful, Stirring, Inspirational Poem of Hope for the Nation

Run Your Business in Ten Essentials for 365 Days and Beyond

www.ingramcontent.com/pod-product-compliance
Lightning Source LLC
LaVergne TN
LVHW072118060526
838201LV00068B/4915